200 no-work
garden ideas

200 no-work garden ideas

hamlyn **all color**

Joanna Smith

An Hachette UK company
www.hachette.co.uk

First published in Great Britain in 2009 by Hamlyn,
a division of Octopus Publishing Group Ltd
2–4 Heron Quays, London E14 4JP
www.octopusbooksusa.com

Distributed in the U.S. and Canada by Octopus Books USA:
c/o Hachette Book Group
237 Park Avenue
New York NY 10017

ISBN: 978-0-600-62035-8

Printed and bound in China

1 2 3 4 5 6 7 8 9 10

contents

introduction

Gardens play a very different role in today's society from 20 years ago. For most people, a garden is no longer a yard in which they can grow some vegetables, raise some prize roses, and spend an industrious retirement. These days, gardening is a means to an end: people want the final result—a pleasant outdoor space for relaxing and entertaining. However, most people don't enjoy the process of achieving that end, and the less work involved, the better.

The no-work garden—a garden that practically looks after itself—might seem an impossible ideal, but we are getting closer to that dream. Advances in gardening science and technology are concentrating on reducing the amount of work we have to do in the garden. Plants are becoming more resistant to diseases, and even the processes of fertilizing and watering plants are becoming automated. And here, to save you even more time, are scores of ingenious ideas.

Of course, the beautiful, flower-filled gardens you see in glossy magazines and on television don't create themselves. Most involve one person, or whole teams, working flat out for hours and hours, day after day. If you're a busy person, how can you ever compete? But having limited time doesn't mean you can't achieve a wonderful garden with a strong, stylish design. There are all kinds of inventive ways to create an imaginative, attractive space without major work. The no-work garden should be a homely, relaxed place where you don't feel guilty every time you see a weed. It's not just a concept but an active state of mind. Something you want to achieve. And can.

Imagine being able to relax in your yard rather than having to work in it. By adopting just a few of the ideas in this book, you will be able to create a space that's virtually self-sufficient. Forget about guilt and inadequacy. Get out your hammock and enjoy your garden!

vertical elements

3 easy-care boundary solutions

walls

A wall is the ultimate no-maintenance boundary and if properly constructed will last for years. There are many styles available, from natural stone to brick or cinder blocks. Choose a material to suit the style of your house and garden, aiming for a neutral backdrop to the planting that will not date over the years or jar if you want to change the design. If you are planning a long wall, why not use a number of complementary materials to add interest or introduce a subtle pattern into the way the bricks or blocks are configured?

fences

A fence is the quickest and easiest barrier to erect, and the job can be tackled by anyone with basic DIY skills. Fences can offer good privacy if you opt for a close-board or panel fence, or they can provide more lightweight yard dividers if you choose a picket or post-and-rail fence. Once erected, a pressure-treated hardwood fence will remain in prime condition for a long time. Wood suits a wide range of styles, ranging from traditional to modern and from rural to urban.

easy-care hedges

"Living" boundaries are often the most visually attractive kind and offer the best solution to blocking out noise and pollution. It is vital to choose the right type of hedge if you want an easy-care boundary. Select your hedge plants according to how often you are willing to trim them. Also consider whether a hedge is evergreen (giving year-round privacy) or deciduous (giving summer-only privacy). Hedges take some years to mature but are worth the wait. Erect a temporary boundary, such as a cheap panel fence, to provide privacy while the hedge grows.

10 no-fuss hedge plants

The following plants are tough and reliable and need clipping just once a year to form a handsome hedge.

1 *Carpinus betulus* (hornbeam)

2 *Corylus avellana* (hazel)

3 *Cotoneaster lacteus*

4 *Crataegus monogyna* (singleseed hawthorn)

5 *Fagus sylvatica* (European beech)

6 *Garrya elliptica* (silk-tassel bush)

7 *Ilex aquifolium* (English holly)

8 *Pyracantha rogersiana* (firethorn)

9 *Taxus baccata* (English yew)

10 *Thuja plicata* (western red cedar)

save time mower power

Deciduous trees create seasonal interest in the garden. In winter, they form a tracery of bare branches against the sky; in spring, the bright green shoots light up the garden; in summer, they provide a soft, leafy backdrop; and, in the fall, many species turn beautiful shades of red and orange. The only downside is the falling leaves, which create great soggy, rotting drifts all over the yard. Forget about hours of laborious sweeping and raking; the quickest way to collect fallen leaves from the lawn, deck, or patio is with the lawn mower. Set the mower to its highest setting and use it to suck up the leaves into its bagging attachment.

8 care-free trees for small yards

Specimen trees should earn their place in the yard, so choose plants with more than one season of interest or that look good year-round. Select easy-care specimens that don't need pruning or special attention. The following trees look after themselves if correctly planted.

1 *Arbutus unedo* (strawberry tree)

2 *Betula utilis* var. *jacquemontii* (white-barked Himalayan birch)

3 *Crataegus laevigata* 'Paul's Scarlet' (English hawthorn)

4 *Ilex* x *altaclerensis* 'Golden King' (holly)

5 *Malus* x *zumi* 'Golden Hornet' (crabapple)

6 *Prunus serrula* (ornamental cherry)

7 *Robinia pseudoacacia* 'Frisia' (black locust)

8 *Sorbus aria* 'Lutescens' (whitebeam)

8 easy-care flowering hedges

Informal hedges need less clipping than formal ones, and the following have the bonus of flowers.

1 *Berberis darwinii* (barberry)

2 *Berberis thunbergii* (Japanese barberry)

3 *Escallonia rubra* 'Crimson Spire'

4 *Forsythia* x *intermedia*

5 *Prunus spinosa* (blackthorn)

6 *Ribes sanguineum* (flowering currant)

7 *Rosa* 'Nevada'

8 *Rosa rugosa* (hedgehog rose)

save time easier hedge cutting

Even if it happens only once a year, the prospect of cutting hedges is unwelcome. But there are some ways to make it quicker and easier. Keep access clear by making sure that there are no other plants growing close to the hedge. If you can maneuver freely, the job is that much simpler. Lay a sheet of plastic or tarp on the ground where you are working, to collect the trimmings and save raking up. And be sure to use a decent hedge trimmer, the best you can afford. It makes a huge difference if you have a long-bladed trimmer that can pass over the top of the hedge in one easy sweep.

3 ideas for easy-care arbors

rustic poles

Perfect for a rural setting or an informal urban yard, rustic poles are easy to work with and can make a sturdy and attractive arbor. Always choose poles that have been pressure treated with preservative, and it'll be a long time before they need any maintenance. Set the uprights in concrete in the ground and cut simple joints where the poles meet, to make a neat fit. Rustic poles can be left in their natural color, and they will take on a neutral silvery hue as they age, or paint them with colored woodstain to complement their surroundings.

sawn hardwood

For a smarter arbor in an urban or contemporary setting, buy an arbor kit with ready-cut uprights and beams that can be quickly bolted together. Be sure to choose pressure-treated hardwood, because softwood will need to be retreated with a preservative every year, and always use galvanized brackets and bolts, to prevent rusting. That way the arbor will not need any care for many years. These kits are simple to erect, especially when attached to one side of a house, where they have a pleasing architectural quality.

brick and rope

Bricks make a handsome and easy-care base for an overhead structure and are attractive in a formal setting. Either hire a professional to build the base or do it yourself: it is a straightforward job for anyone with practical skills. The brick base can be linked by swags of thick, synthetic rope in a neutral shade. Alternatively, use chains or wooden beams. A brick-and-rope arbor suits an urban garden, but, if appropriate, be sure to match the bricks to those used to build the house.

quick fix simple cover-up

Although a tree lives a long time, it will eventually die and leave you with a potentially large, unattractive stump. Instead of removing it, convert the stump into an eye-catching feature by training a vine over it. Choose an easy-care vine, such as *Clematis montana* var. *rubens*, which will be covered with pretty, pink blooms in spring, or honeysuckle, with its lovely scent.

hired help

Birds can be a great help in the garden, eating insect pests, such as aphids and caterpillars, and devouring slugs and snails. The best way to attract them is by planting trees in which they can nest and feed. Those with fruits and berries are always a magnet, with rowan (*Sorbus aucuparia*) and crabapples, such as *Malus* x *zumi* 'Golden Hornet', popular choices. Holly is another winner, but be sure to plant both a male and female plant to make sure there are plenty of berries.

quick fix
from dull
to daring

Large expanses of plain fence or trellis can look dull, and the solution is to cover them with vines, but they do need time and effort while they are growing. A quicker and easier makeover can be achieved with just a coat of colored woodstain. This can really transform a fence and the garden, creating a different look for very little effort. Choose a water-based product, to make cleaning up easier, and pick a shade to suit the garden. Soft pastels, such as silvery blue, sage-green, or primrose, will create a subtle backdrop to soft planting, adding an oasis of calm. Vibrant shades, such as red, bright blue, or golden yellow, inject a bold statement and need to be used with care. Don't feel restricted by just one color: a fence or trellis can be given even more personality by combining two or more shades.

3 things to avoid

climbing roses

Most roses should be avoided by the no-work gardener. Not only do they need pruning and regular summer deadheading to perform well, but many are susceptible to pests and diseases, such as blackspot, creating even more work. Climbing roses are worse, because they need a support to climb up, and you have to tie the individual branches and new shoots to this structure as they grow. In addition, there's the difficulty of pruning several feet above ground, which invariably involves a ladder.

tall, vigorous hedges

Fast-growing conifers are perfect for creating an almost instant hedge, as they grow so fast in the first few years. The leyland cypress (x *Cupressocyparis leylandii*) puts on 3½ ft. (1 m) a year for the first 20 years or so, but despite slowing up it still grows at 2 ft. (60 cm) a year, eventually reaching 115 ft. (35 m). The only way to keep such sprinters in check is to trim the hedge two or three times a year, so choose your hedge plants with care. Even privet needs cutting twice a year.

untreated softwood structures

It is tempting to choose softwood poles, posts, and boards to make fences, arches, and other structures for the garden, as they are cheaper and easier to work with than hardwood. There are also many kits available for overhead structures such as arbors and arches made from softwood, which seem like good value. But they are a false economy. Not only will you have to treat the entire structure with a coat of wood preservative every year, but you will also have to replace the structure when the wood rots after just a few years. Pressure-treated hardwood does not need this attention.

save time choose the right plant ties

Instead of fiddling with short lengths of twine that are tricky to cut and handle, buy easy-to-use plant ties to save time when tying climbing plants to a trellis or overhead structure. There are many different types available, including stiff, plastic ties that work like a belt and plastic-coated wire on a convenient dispenser, which is quick and simple to use. Perhaps the easiest are the "Velcro" plant ties.

8 care-free plants for walls, fences, and arbors

When you are choosing plants to clothe your vertical surfaces, pick those that require little pruning and maintenance to stay looking good throughout the year.

1 *Actinidia kolomikta*

2 *Clematis montana*

3 *Hedera helix* (English ivy)

4 *Humulus lupulus* 'Aureus' (golden hop)

5 *Hydrangea anomala* subsp. *petiolaris* (climbing hydrangea)

6 *Jasminum officinale* (jasmine)

7 *Lonicera periclymenum* (honeysuckle)

8 *Parthenocissus quinquefolia* (Virginia creeper)

2 ideas for no-fuss fences

closeboard fence

Closeboard fences are made from a series of wooden boards nailed vertically to a framework. As they are usually constructed *in situ*, they can be made to any height and are well suited to sloping ground. The closely arranged boards offer good privacy and make an attractive boundary. Closeboard fences should last a long time without any maintenance, provided you use pressure-treated hardwood.

panel fence

Panel fences are made from a series of preconstructed panels, making them quick and easy to erect. The panels are formed from very thin strips of wood attached to a rectangular framework, and they are available in a number of different sizes. They offer good privacy but are not especially attractive. They can, however, be made more sympathetic if you paint them with woodstain or use a covering of easy-care vines. Choose good-quality panels if you want them to last, and make sure that they have been pressure treated with preservative.

2 more ideas for no-fuss fences

picket fence

Picket fences are made from a series of flat, wooden uprights nailed, with spaces between them, to horizontal rails. They can be made *in situ* from individual boards, while the speedier option is to buy preconstructed panels. Picket fences are certainly charming but offer little privacy, because they are usually quite low and the boards are well spaced out. They are perfect for front lawns, where privacy is not required, or as a lightweight boundary between two different areas of the yard. Choose pressure-treated lumber, preferably hardwood, to cut down on maintenance.

post and rail

Post-and-rail fences are made from rustic poles and lend a distinctly rural touch. They are quick and inexpensive to erect and are ideal in a rural yard where they won't block out any views (which also means they won't provide any privacy). They also make effective garden dividers. As with other fences, use poles that have been pressure treated with a preservative, so that you won't have to replace rotting posts every few years.

quick fix
big impact, little work

Plants make the garden an attractive and relaxing space, but, for the no-work gardener, extra borders mean extra time and effort. For maximum visual impact without all the maintenance that a new border entails, try erecting a simple arbor (see page 18) and training an easy-care vine over it. Use rustic poles or a simple kit to construct a basic arbor, and choose one of the undemanding vines listed below to cover it and you'll only have to tuck in the odd wayward stem.

8 easy-care vines

The following vines will readily climb up a support without the need for training. They are all reliable, easy to grow, and require little maintenance.

1 *Clematis alpina* (alpine clematis)

2 *Clematis macropetala*

3 *Humulus lupulus* 'Aureus' (golden hop)

4 *Jasminum beesianum* (jasmine)

5 *Jasminum officinale* 'Argenteovariegatum' (jasmine)

6 *Lonicera sempervirens* (coral honeysuckle)

7 *Parthenocissus henryana* (Chinese Virginia creeper)

8 *Passiflora caerulea* (blue passionflower)

brightening a featureless wall

reflecting space

Walls are the perfect boundary for the no-work garden, but a large expanse of wall can be dominating, and a high wall can make a small space feel claustrophobic. Try fixing a large mirror to a wall to give the illusion of space and to break up an otherwise featureless boundary. The effect looks best when the edges of the mirror are hidden, perhaps by using climbing plants on the wall or bushy shrubs right in front of it or by placing a wooden arch around it to give the illusion that it is a doorway.

pots of interest

Instead of creating a border in front of a wall to introduce some color, fix a series of pots to the wall at various heights to create interest where it is really needed and to cut down on the extra work. Choose specially designed wall pots with a flat side, window boxes, or standard flower pots fixed to the wall with wire or metal collars. Keep in mind that the pots will dry out quickly in such a place, especially against a sunny wall, so choose the largest pots that are practical and line porous ones with plastic to help retain moisture and minimize the amount of watering. Choose drought-resistant plants that require little attention, such as sempervivums, thrift, sedum, and pelargoniums.

trellis

Trellis offers a great way to add interest to a dull wall or fence and without the maintenance of growing climbing plants. Trellis comes in panels of all shapes and sizes, with a range of decorative designs. Choose shallow panels with undulating top edges to fit above a featureless wall or fence, or screw decorative panels to a surface to add pattern and texture. Colorful paints and woodstain can be used to great effect if you paint the trellis a different color from the backing wall or fence.

right plant, right spot

Before selecting a tree for the garden or a climbing plant to cover a fence, wall, or arbor, always check the conditions where the plant is to grow so that you can pick a plant that will be happy there. Check how much sun it will get. Will it be in an exposed or sheltered site? Is the soil moist or dry, acidic or alkaline? The better suited a plant is to the conditions in which it is growing, the healthier it will be without your help. If it struggles to survive in an inhospitable spot, it will succumb to pests and diseases, making more work for you. A happy plant means an owner with time to relax.

save time
perfect
planting

Follow these simple guidelines for planting trees and hedges, to avoid future problems and the need to cosset unhappy plants. Get it right from the start and the work will end there.

• Plant trees and hedges in the fall, when the ground is moist, and water them well. Winter rains should keep them moist enough without the need for further watering. Water young plants well in hot dry spells over summer until they are well established.

• Prepare the soil well, to make sure the plants get a good start. Break up the soil in the base of the planting hole, to aid drainage, and mix plenty of well-rotted organic matter into the soil, to retain moisture.

• Mix a handful of slow-release fertilizer into the soil when planting, to encourage the tree to grow well.

• Make sure that you get the planting depth right— plants go into the ground at the same depth as they were in their containers.

• Keep checking that your tree or hedge looks healthy. If the weather is very dry and you do need to water, provide a big drink to encourage the plant to produce deep rather than shallow roots, to make it more resistant to drought in the future.

care-free surfaces

2 easy-care surfaces

paving slabs

Paving slabs are the ultimate in low-maintenance surfaces: if properly laid, they will outlast several garden owners. There are many different styles available, from beautiful, natural stone to some realistic man-made alternatives, as well as chic, contemporary designs. Slabs come in a range of shapes and sizes that can be mixed, to add interest. Paving slabs are a relatively expensive option if you hire someone to lay them, but they are attractive, hard wearing, and maintenance free. The base needs to be thoroughly prepared and the gaps must be pointed with mortar.

bricks

Like paving slabs, bricks offer a durable and long-lasting walkway surface with no care required. They create a pleasing, busy effect, which is perfect for small areas of patio or service paths, or you could try combining bricks with slabs, to add visual interest. Bricks can also be laid in a number of attractive patterns, including herringbone and basketweave. Be sure to use frost-proof paving bricks, and point the gaps between the bricks with mortar, to stop any weeds growing through.

2 more easy-care surfaces

hardwood decks

A deck is made from softer material than paving, both physically and visually. It is ideal if you want to raise the level of the ground, and it can be built on a slope or an uneven surface without the need for exhausting and time-consuming leveling. To be low maintenance, the deck must be made from pressure-treated hardwood lumber, so that it will last for many years with no further treatment. Although it is expensive, a wooden deck is a very effective, long-lasting, low-maintenance surface.

gravel

Gravel is a neutral material that looks good in any situation, whether it's a traditional rural setting, a Mediterranean-style garden, or a modern, urban yard. It is quicker and cheaper to lay than most other surfaces and gives a more natural look than paving slabs or wood. Gravel is also a flexible option that can be used to cover any shape, while you can grow plants in it if you need a softer look. There is a wide range of gravels, including pea gravel (rounded stones in shades of brown and cream), limestone or granite chips that come in a choice of colors, slate chippings, and larger pebbles.

5 high-maintenance features to avoid

- Grass pathways—the edges need clipping regularly and the grass gets concentrated wear, leading to unsightly bald patches. Grass pathways are also tricky to mow.

- Small, shady lawns—grass never grows well in shade, and a small lawn gets walked on so much that it will never look any good.

- Gravel with no underlying landscape fabric—gravel that's walked on regularly and is pressed into the soil seems to offer the perfect conditions for germinating weed seeds.

- Plants spilling over lawn edges—mowing is made more difficult, and the plants will soon kill the grass as they cover it with shade, leading to ugly, bare patches that need repairing.

- Gaps in paving—weeds will soon take hold and are difficult to remove without recourse to herbicides.

quick fix
instant lawn

When laying a new patch of lawn, use sod instead of sowing seed. Sod gives instant results, and you don't have to wait for it to grow while fighting off hungry birds. Choose large sods, preferably in long rolls, because they take less time to lay. Also water the ground thoroughly before laying the sods, and keep them moist until well established. If they dry out they will shrink, and gaps will appear between them. If this does happen, fill the gaps with sifted soil and grass seed and make sure that the grass is kept moist.

save time
the right
mower

Using the right tools makes a job easier, and mowing is no exception. Choose a mower to suit your lawn and the type of cut you want. Reel mowers are perfect for neat, level lawns and give a fine cut, while a rotary mower will be easier to push across uneven ground and areas of rough grass. Electric mowers are cheap and convenient, but you must keep the cable well away, to avoid getting it sliced by the cutters (and use a circuit interrupter, to eliminate the risk of electric shocks). Gas-driven mowers are better for large areas of grass, but they are more expensive to buy. For the ultimate in labor-saving devices, buy a robotic mower, which will mow the lawn for you. Just secure a wire around the edges of your lawn, and the battery-driven device will keep the grass beautifully clipped while you watch.

3 ideas for easy-care pathways

perfect pavers

Long-lasting manufactured pavers are the easiest surface to care for. There is a wide range of different paving slabs, many of which make an attractive walkway. They can, however, be expensive to lay, and larger slabs of 18 in. (45 cm) or more will work only on a straight walkways: choose smaller slabs for curvy ones, to avoid too much cutting. Prepare the base using a good depth of rubble and sand—3 in. (8 cm) and 2 in. (5 cm) respectively—as a walkway gets heavy use. Point between the slabs with mortar, to discourage weeds.

bricks and Belgian blocks

Like pavers, bricks and Belgian blocks make a hardwearing walkway that requires no maintenance. Although they are fiddlier to lay than pavers, the smaller units lend themselves to the small scale of a path and are easier to arrange in curves. Both bricks and Belgian blocks should be laid on a firm base of rubble. Instead of pointing the gaps with wet mortar, brush a dry mixture of sand and cement over the path, to fill the gaps, and then water it in.

gravel

Gravel paths are cheap and flexible to lay and easy to maintain. Gravel can be used to make a path of any shape or size, and it looks good in a range of different settings. To make a long-lasting path, lay the gravel on a base of compacted rubble, and firm the gravel down into it, to make an impenetrable base. This will keep the gravel in place and make the path more comfortable to walk on. You need to contain the rubble and gravel within metal strips or wooden boards, held in place by stakes, on each side of the path.

quick fix
lawn fertilizer

For a lush and healthy lawn in one quick step, apply a combined weed-and-fertilize product to the lawn in the fall or spring. If the grass is kept healthy, the lawn will be less susceptible to weeds and will be better able to resist drought, saving you time and energy while making the lawn look great. Simply sprinkle the weed-and-fertilize mix over the lawn when rain is forecast, and let nature wash it in. If there is no rain in the next three days or so, water it in with a hose and sprinkler.

easy-care
lawns

When laying a new lawn, whether it's sod or seed, choose an easy-care utility grass mix that contains rye. Although the resulting lawn will not be as velvety as a fine grass mixture, it will be much tougher and will withstand more wear, which is especially important if you have children or pets. Warm-season grasses such as Bermuda grass and zoysia are more resistant to drought than cool-season ones, so you won't have to water the lawn in dry weather.

weed-free gravel

Areas of gravel can be infested with weeds in no time, but there is a simple solution. Lay a weed-suppressing landscape fabric under the gravel, and you'll never have to weed again. This semi-permeable fabric allows water to penetrate into the soil while stopping weeds from growing through it. You can, though, insert the occasional plant in the gravel to soften the effect: simply brush back the gravel, cut a cross in the fabric, and peel back the four flaps. After planting, replace the fabric and gravel. If you aren't planning to do any planting, use thick polyethylene instead: it will suppress weeds in the same way but is cheaper.

replacing broken slabs

Broken paving slabs are a problem. They look unsightly and you might trip over them, but replacing the whole patio is a daunting prospect. Instead, replace just the broken slabs with a different material, to save time. There are many options, including bricks, Belgian blocks, pebbles, or pieces of broken tile arranged in a mosaic. Remove the broken slabs using a hammer and brick-set chisel, and if necessary chip away the mortar beneath, to accommodate the new material. Set the replacement bricks, tiles, or pebbles into a layer of wet mortar and allow it to harden, pointing later if necessary.

2 ideas to make mowing easier

rationalize the shape

Is your mowing made more complicated by the need to reverse in and out of tight corners and negotiate tricky bends? If so, simplify the shape of your lawn to reduce the amount of time spent mowing. A rectangle or circle is the easiest option, but a more free-form shape is fine if you stick to sweeping curves and avoid island beds, grass paths, and awkward extensions to the lawn.

avoid obstacles

Obstacles in the lawn, including shrubs, trees, garden benches, tubs and other containers, make mowing more time consuming. They also stop the lawn looking particularly neat, as there will always be long, straggly bits of grass around the obstacle that the mower cannot reach. So clear the lawn of all obstacles, or stand a bench or container on a square of paving that has been set into the lawn at the same level as the grass, so that the mower can skim over the top of it.

quick fix
seating area on sloping ground

To avoid heavy groundwork and having to level sloping ground for a seating area, create a wooden deck.
A deck is ideal on uneven or sloping ground, as the boards are attached to a subframe that stands on wooden piers. Each pier can be made longer or shorter as necessary, to accommodate the different levels.
If the deck is above ground level, build a balustrade around the edge for safety, with steps up to allow easy access. The balustrade and steps should be planned as part of the overall structure. Use strong, pressure-treated lumber when building the frame, because it lasts a long time. The area under the deck can be used as storage space, perhaps for trashcans or stacks of flower pots.

complete freedom

With all the effort involved in mowing, fertilizing, and watering lawns in dry weather, ask yourself if you really need one. Many small yards would be better without grass altogether, particularly those in shade or the ones that get a lot of wear, because grass simply won't thrive in these conditions. Unless you have young children, opt for another more practical and hardwearing surface, such as gravel, and relish your mower-free days.

quick fix from grass to shredded hardwood

Grass pathways are the no-work gardener's worst enemy, so why not replace them right away? The quickest and cheapest solution is to use a shredded wood mulch, which is quick and easy to lay, creating an informal, natural path that is perfect for a shady garden. It is essential to lay thick polyethylene under the shredded wood, to prevent weeds from growing through it. You could use a weed-suppressing landscape fabric, but it will be more expensive than polyethylene, and you don't need to let moisture permeate through it. Shredded wood is comfortable to walk on and provides a soft landing for small children.

the bigger the better

The bigger the area of hard surface, the easier it is to maintain, but large areas of pavers or gravel can look dull and featureless. You could soften the effect with borders or containers or an area of lawn, but that involves hard work. Instead, make the hard surface more varied so that it is interesting in its own right, avoiding the need for extra features. Try combining areas of pavers, bricks, Belgian blocks, gravel, or wooden decking material, or choose two or three contrasting materials that complement the style of your house. Consider an area of cream pavers surrounded by a band of gray ones, with an area of gravel toward the end of the backyard. Plant a few architectural plants in the gravel and add some garden ornaments.

creative concrete

Poured concrete is the ultimate low-maintenance surface, and one that is quick and cheap to achieve. It's a very contemporary material that's popular with designers and doesn't have to be a sea of battleship gray. It can be colored to create various effects, while the surface can be ridged, smooth, or rough, depending on how it is treated after it has been laid. Alternatively, an aggregate, such as gravel, can be set into it.

save time
add an
edging strip

Trimming lawn edges is one of the most time-consuming and unnecessary jobs in the garden. To avoid ever having to do it again, create a mowing strip around your lawn to stop the grass from growing into any surrounding borders. Set lengths of 4 in. (10 cm) square, pressure-treated lumber into the ground around the edges of the lawn, with the top of the lumber flush with the grass. Then drive stakes into the border, to hold the lumber in place. The lawn mower will simply pass over the lumber. Alternatively, use bricks or paving slabs set in mortar to edge the grass, again setting them flush with the lawn. Bricks are useful for lawns with curved edges, and paving slabs are a good choice if your plants spill out of the borders.

halve the mowing

If you don't have a lot of spare time, ask yourself if you need to mow the whole lawn. Areas of long grass can look very attractive, creating a cool, leafy look. So mow the grass closest to the house to give space for sitting out and children's games, and leave the rest as meadow. You may even get some wild flowers in the long grass if you cut it just twice a year—once in early spring and once in late summer.

raising the cut

Cutting a lawn very short on a regular basis stresses the grass and weakens it. This makes it more susceptible to drought in dry weather and means it is more likely to be colonized by moss, both of which lead to an unsightly lawn that needs attention to keep it in shape. Raise the height of your mower blades to keep your lawn healthy: it should still be leafy and green, even after it has just been mown.

save time
lay walkways
correctly

Paved areas should last for many years—whether they are made of manufactured pavers, flagstones, bricks, or Belgian blocks—but only if they have been correctly laid. Poorly laid walkways will soon start to break up and weeds will emerge, leaving you with an even bigger problem than you initially faced. Follow these four simple pointers:

• Choose frost-proof paving materials. Some bricks and tiles will crumble if they freeze, leading to an uneven and unsightly surface that will have to be replaced.

• Lay all paving units on a slight slope to allow water to drain away when it rains. This avoids the problem of standing water and is particularly important if the walkway is next to the house.

• Construct a firm base. You will need at least 6 in. (15 cm) of compacted rubble, topped with at least 2 in. (5 cm) of compacted sand on which to set the mortar and slabs. Alternatively, make a plinth of poured concrete at least 4 in. (10 cm) deep and lay the paving materials on top.

• Point the gaps between the paving units with mortar, to make sure that no weeds can grow there. Not only do weeds look unsightly but also their roots will start to break up the walkway.

quick fix
instant
cover-up

A fast way to rejuvenate a tired, old patio is simply to cover it with decking material. This means you don't have to dig up the rubble base or worry about a damp-proof course. These preconstructed wooden squares, usually 18–24 in. (45–60 cm) across, make an attractive surface that can be stained any color or be left natural, to suit your garden. The patio can be used as a firm, level surface on which to set the decking pieces. Simply screw them to a subframe of evenly spaced lengths of square lumber laid on the patio, so that the deck forms a floating raft on top. It's that simple.

save time
a deck
to last

A good deck will last many years without maintenance, so it is well worth investing the time and money to make it as strong and durable as possible.

- Use heavy, pressure-treated lumber, 4–6 in. (10–15 cm) square, for the subframe.

- Set the uprights in concrete and chamfer the top of the concrete around the posts, to allow rainwater to run away. This should give better rot protection than the metal post supports that hold the posts in constant contact with the soil.

- Use hardwood for the deck, as it doesn't need any further coats of preservative.

- Buy galvanized screws, bolts, and brackets, to avoid rust.

replacing a lawn in shade

shredded hardwood

Small, shady lawns rarely look good: the grass is usually thin and drawn, leaving it susceptible to bald patches and moss. Shredded hardwood mulch makes a pleasing, natural-looking alternative that suits the feel of a shady garden. Simply slice off the turf with a spade, lay a weed-suppressing landscape fabric over the soil, and top it with a 4 in. (10 cm) layer of shredded wood. Add an edging strip around the area, to keep the mulch in place. You won't have to weed or mow again.

cocoa shells

Crushed cocoa shells are an attractive alternative and give a smarter appearance than shredded wood. Cocoa shells look like shiny, dark brown flakes, and, because they set off plants beautifully, grow a few shade-loving specimen trees and shrubs in the mulch. They also smell delicious! Lay the cocoa shells in the same way as shredded hardwood. Because you no longer need to mow, you can stand a garden bench, a few easy-care tubs, or garden ornaments on the shredded hardwood or cocoa shells, to add extra stylish features.

making life easier

2 ideas to make weeding easier

little but often

Weeds are easiest to deal with when they are small. If you catch them when they are seedlings, annual weeds can be quickly tugged out of the soil with a hoe, while perennial weeds are also much easier to remove, roots and all, to prevent any regrowth. Get into the habit of a quick weed patrol once a week, to prevent them taking hold. If they have a chance to spread, they'll end up posing a serious problem that will take many hours with a spade to remedy. And if you let them flower and then set seed, you will have a really serious battle on your hands. Nip the problem in the bud, to save yourself many hours of hard work later.

weed after rain

The easiest time to weed is after rain when the soil is still moist. Weed roots can be removed without difficulty, and you are less likely to miss a section of perennial weed root that could quickly regrow. Use a hand fork to loosen the soil, and then pull the weed gently but firmly, and it should come out intact.

save time
use a
soaker hose

A soaker hose is a good way to water a newly planted area until the plants have become established, and it will save you hours with the watering can. After planting, lay the soaker hose around the plants, and then put a mulch over the top, to hide the hose and stop the water evaporating. When the hose is switched on, water seeps gently out through the walls of the hose into the surrounding soil. If your plants are spaced out, use a similar irrigation system but with individual "drippers" at intervals along a pipe. For added convenience, fit a timer to the faucet, so that the water comes on automatically each evening for an hour or so, and then you won't have to think about watering any more.

water
thoroughly

The deeper water penetrates into the ground, the deeper a plant's roots will grow. That means it'll be less susceptible to drought in the future, saving you the effort of watering it further. Should you water a little and often instead, then the roots will stay near the soil surface to get what little moisture there is. In times of drought, these plants with shallow roots will be the worst affected, because the soil surface dries out first. When you water a plant, always water it thoroughly.

clear weeds before planting

Before introducing new plants, clear the soil very thoroughly of weeds. This is particularly important with perennial weeds, because they are extremely difficult to remove when they are growing up through other plants and their roots are entwined. Dig the soil thoroughly and remove every piece of weed root before planting.

8 perennial weeds

Perennial weeds are a gardener's worst enemy. Here are the most common culprits.

1 Ground elder, bishop's weed (*Aegopodium podagraria*)

2 Oxalis, wood sorrel (*Oxalis* spp.)

3 Bindweed (*Calystegia* spp., *Convolvulus* spp.)

4 Horsetail (*Equisetum arvense*)

5 Dandelion (*Taraxacum officinale*)

6 Quackgrass, couchgrass (*Agropyron repens*)

7 Ground ivy (*Glechoma hederacea*)

8 Kudzu (*Pueraria lobata*)

quick fix
call in the
cavalry

If you simply don't have the time or energy to tackle a large job, such as laying a patio, felling a tree, or replacing your lawn with shredded wood mulch for an easier life, employ someone to do it for you. There are many specialty firms and general horticulturalists with the expertise and right tools who will take on such work. Choose a company based on personal recommendation and ask for a written estimate before the work starts. It is vital to check that the company has adequate insurance for the tasks being quoted. You may also want to employ a casual gardener to keep a regular eye on the garden if you feel it's getting the upper hand.

garden
clear-up

Aesthetic considerations aside, there are many practical reasons why it's important to keep the garden tidy. Piles of debris, such as old flower pots, garbage bags, and cardboard boxes, offer the perfect environment in which slugs and snails can live and breed—they really don't need encouraging—so get rid of the debris. It's also important to dispose of organic matter, such as prunings, weeds, and dead plants, which might harbor viruses and other diseases and pass them on to your plants. It pays to keep tidying up. Remember not to add diseased plant material to your compost pile, in case the viruses and bacteria are not killed during the composting process.

save time
mulch, mulch and, more mulch

Mulches are the mainstay of the no-work garden. Organic mulches, using materials such as well-rotted compost or leafmold, are particularly beneficial and work in three ways:

- They suppress weed growth, reducing the hours you need to spend weeding.

- They conserve moisture in the soil, cutting down the time spent watering.

- They are gradually incorporated into the soil, improving the structure and nutrient levels, which means you get healthier plants that don't need so much fertilizing.

Apply organic mulch to the garden each spring, when the soil is moist and warm. Avoid piling it up around plant stems or they may rot, but aim to cover all the bare soil. Worms will gradually take it down into the ground, so provide an annual top-up.

3 ideas for organic mulches

well-rotted compost

Compost is a crumbly, brown material that is created by rotting organic matter. Many people have a compost pile or bin in which to recycle their kitchen and garden waste, but if you don't make compost yourself you can buy it in bags from garden centers. Don't worry about weed seeds. Even if they are thrown onto the pile, they will be killed when the compost heats up to 140°F (60°C) while rotting. Spread the mulch in the garden to a depth of 4–6 in. (10–15 cm) in late spring. The ideal time is when the soil has started to warm up but is still moist after the winter rains.

composted bark

Composted bark is, as the name suggests, partially rotted bark chips, but it is chunkier than compost and makes a better weed-suppressant, as do hardwood chips. Since both these take longer to be incorporated into the soil, you may need to top them up only every other year. Although they provide fewer nutrients than compost, they are still worthwhile.

well-rotted manure

When rotted down, animal manure is dark and crumbly with a pleasant smell, and it makes a great mulch. It is rich in nutrients and helps retain moisture in the soil. Manure on straw bedding is the best kind, because the straw will be full of urine, and it rots down more quickly than wood chips. Never use fresh manure as a mulch, because it will scorch the plants and rob them of nutrients as it rots.

2 more organic mulches

mushroom compost

Spent compost from commercial mushroom growers also makes a suitable mulch and can be obtained fairly cheaply. It is dark and fibrous, a mixture of animal manure, peat moss, and gypsum. As the compost is alkaline, do not use it near acid-loving plants such as rhododendrons. Spread it 4–6 in. (10–15 cm) thick in the garden in late spring, avoiding any plant stems.

leafmold

If you have deciduous trees overhanging your yard, they can be used as a free and convenient source of leafmold for mulching. There are two ways in which to make leafmold. The first is to place the leaves in black garbage bags and tie their tops. Then make a few holes in each bag, place the bags in a corner, and leave them for a year. The second involves piling the leaves into a simple cage made of wire netting, to contain them, and leaving them to rot for at least a year. Leafmold contains fewer nutrients than compost or manure, but it is still extremely good for the soil and makes a useful mulch.

useful amphibians

Frogs and toads will help clear the garden of slugs and snails. Provide them with a pond and somewhere to spend the winter. Create an inviting pile of logs or stones in a rough corner of the yard surrounded by undergrowth or in the back of the flower garden in the shade, and they will soon move in.

no digging

Not only is digging hard work but it can also bring fresh weed seeds to the surface where the daylight will help them germinate. Adopt a no-dig system by preparing the soil thoroughly before planting a new area, and then leave it alone. Apply an organic mulch each year, to fertilize the soil and improve its structure, and promptly remove any weeds that pop through. But don't turn the soil over again, except when planting.

keep plants well fertilized

Plants need nutrients to grow and flower well and to help them shrug off pest and disease attacks. Treat the soil with a slow-release fertilizer in the spring, forking it into the surface. This takes very little time and effort, but the rewards will be great. Don't apply too much fertilizer, or the plants will become soft and sappy and a magnet for pests.

be vigilant

Most pest and disease problems are easy to eradicate if you catch them early. Take a stroll around the garden once a week or so, and keep an eye out for nibbled leaves, distorted stems, or anything out of the ordinary. If you do spot a problem, deal with it straight away before the plant gets stressed or the problem spreads to neighboring plants. An isolated case is much easier to deal with than a major outbreak.

save time
blast those
aphids

A quick, easy, and satisfying way to deal with an infestation of aphids on your plants is to blast them away with the hose. Simply spray them off affected stems with a jet of water and they shouldn't return. Periodically check the plant and others close by, to check there aren't any more infestations.

2 ideas for free labor

energetic earthworms

Earthworms do a great deal to improve the structure of your soil, and that, in turn, keeps plants healthy and avoids time-consuming problems in the future. As each worm feeds and burrows, so soil passes through its body and is bound into crumbs, and this improves drainage and increases aeration. You can encourage worms into your garden by adding plenty of organic matter to the soil in the form of well-rotted compost or manure. Add it when you are preparing new areas, when planting, and as a mulch. Keep the worms happy, and they will keep your soil in tip-top condition, helping to keep plant problems at bay.

lady beetles and lacewings

Both lady beetles and lacewings are important friends for the no-work gardener, as they feast on surprising quantities of aphids, red spider mites, mealy bugs, whiteflies, scale insects, and all manner of garden pests. Encourage these useful creatures to breed, feed, and overwinter in your garden by buying a special, small, purpose-made "house" for them. Lacewing chambers and lady beetle houses are designed to help these beneficial insects survive through winter, and some houses even have a special viewing window, so you can see just how many you have.

stay sharp

Garden tools that are in good condition make jobs quicker and easier, so keep them in good shape. Have pruning shears and loppers sharpened from time to time, and you'll be amazed at how much easier they are to use. Clean earth off spades, trowels, and forks, to prevent rusting, unless they are stainless steel.

rent the right equipment

It pays to have the right tool for the job: digging takes half the time with a rotary tiller, laying an area of pavers is easy with a cement mixer, and a patch of wilderness can be reclaimed much more quickly with a weedwhacker. When you are planning to tackle a major job in the garden, rent the right equipment to make it simpler. Renting is much cheaper than buying and makes perfect sense for one-off or occasional jobs.

save time buy healthy plants

Sickly or diseased plants are a waste of money and time. If new plants are infected with pests or diseases, they may pass them onto your other plants, and you'll have an infestation. If the new plants are weak or pot-bound, they will either need to be cosseted to be brought back to full health—something you haven't got time for—or they will simply die and you'll have to buy some more. When choosing plants, first check the foliage: is it fresh and healthy? Are there any signs of pests or diseases? Then, if possible, slip the plant out of its pot, and check the roots. There should be a number of healthy-looking roots with plenty of soil between them. If a mat of tangled roots has spread through the base of the pot, the plant has been in its container for too long and won't thrive when it is planted in the garden.

2 ideas for keeping plants healthy

good preparation

Healthy plants are less likely to succumb to pests and diseases, so it makes sense to ensure that your plants stay in the best possible shape. Give them an excellent start by preparing the ground thoroughly before planting. It just takes three steps:

- Dig over the soil and remove all traces of weeds.

- If the soil hasn't been dug before, break it up to a depth of 12–18 in. (30–45 cm), depending on the size of the plant.

- Incorporate organic matter into the soil, such as well-rotted compost or manure, before planting.

good planting technique

Follow these tips to get the right planting technique:

- Start by watering the plant thoroughly in its pot at least one hour before planting. If the rootball is dry, leave the potted plant to soak in a bucket of water for one hour.

- Dig a hole at least 1 in. (2.5 cm) deeper than the plant's rootball and about one-and-a-half times as wide.

- Add extra organic matter at this stage: fork it into the planting hole, and mix it with the soil that is being used to backfill the hole. Add a handful of slow-release fertilizer at the same time.

- Remove the plant from its pot, and plant it at the same depth that it was in its pot.

- Firm the soil around the rootball, and water thoroughly to settle the soil around the roots.

6 worst time-wasters

The following jobs are tedious time-wasters. Aim to eliminate them for a freer, more relaxed lifestyle.

• Digging—this is tiring and unnecessary. Adopt the no-dig system (see page 90).

• Weeding—prevent weeds appearing by using mulches and weed-suppressing landscape fabric and by arranging plants close together so that there's no bare soil where they can thrive (see pages 76, 80, 84 and 106).

• Watering—choose drought-resistant plants, mulch well, and incorporate plenty of organic matter into the soil, to retain moisture. If necessary, use an automatic irrigation system (see page 78).

• Hedge-trimming—choose easy-care hedging plants that need cutting only once a year (see page 12) or erect a fence or wall instead.

• Pruning—avoid shrubs and trees that need pruning to perform well. Instead, choose easy-care plants that look after themselves (see page 114).

• Clipping lawn edges—what could be more time consuming? The quick solution is to edge the lawn with a mowing strip (see page 64).

5 ways to attract birds

Birds are voracious eaters and can quickly consume countless insect pests. Here are five good ways to attract birds into the yard.

- Hang up birdfeeders and offer a selection of foods to attract a wide range of species that eat different pests. Fat feeders, nuts, and seeds are very popular.

- A birdbath, garden pond, or even a bowl of water on the platform bird feeder will give them somewhere to drink and bathe, especially in winter.

- Leave seedheads on ornamental grasses and perennials over winter, because they are loved by finches and other small birds. Don't cut back these plants until next spring.

- Grow shrubs with berries, such as holly and pyracantha, to provide food in winter.

- Use bird houses and dense evergreen shrubs to tempt the birds to stay.

dealing with slugs and snails

slug pub

Fill some old plastic pots or cartons with beer and sink them into the soil, so that the rims are level with the surface. Slugs and snails are attracted to the beer and fall into the traps and drown. Replace the beer from time to time, to keep it fresh. This also works with milk.

fruit skins

Molluscs like somewhere moist to hide during the day, so place some scooped-out orange, grapefruit, or melon skins, outer side down, in the garden among your plants. Check under the skins every morning and dispose of the slugs and snails in a bucket of salt water. Wear a pair of rubber gloves if you're squeamish.

flashlight vigil

Slugs and snails come out at night, and that's the best time to patrol the garden. Go out with a flashlight, collect all the molluscs you can find, and put them in a bucket of salty water.

2 more weed-busting ideas

shade them out

Weed seeds need light to germinate and grow, so pack your plants close together to make sure there are no patches of bare soil that they can colonize. Try choosing several plants of the same species that can be grown close together, to make a large drift. Also put groups of plants that are equally vigorous next to each other—so that none is ever swamped—for the same effect. When growing plants close together, keep the soil nutrient and moisture levels higher than normal so that all the plants can thrive.

prevent attacks from neighbors

If your neighbors are less conscientious about weeding than you are, their perennial weeds might spread into your garden. A fence certainly won't keep out stinging nettles, for example, which spread by underground roots. Make an impenetrable barrier by digging a 12 in. (30 cm) deep trench along the base of the fence. Nail a strip of weed-suppressing landscape fabric or thick black polyethylene to the base of the fence, then push it down into the trench, and replace the soil. That should keep the weeds out.

plant post-mortem

Even if you plant correctly, and fertilize and water regularly, the occasional plant may die. Check it to see what happened. This will alert you to any problems that may affect other plants and give you a chance to treat them before it's too late.

• Check the leaves for signs of damage: have they been nibbled, or can you see any pests lurking there?

• Also check the stems for pests or diseases.

• If you don't find anything, check the roots for pests. Have they been eaten, or have they shriveled, suggesting drought or waterlogging?

• Then check the soil around the roots for grubs, especially soil weevil grubs, or other pests.

• If you can't see anything, ask yourself whether the plant was in the correct position. Was it too dry or too wet for that particular species? Did it have too much sun or not enough? Was the soil too acidic or too alkaline?

no-guilt borders

3 things to avoid

herbaceous perennials

Herbaceous perennials need time and attention to keep them looking good. They die down in the winter months, and the dead stems have to be cut off before new shoots appear next spring. Many perennials also need staking, or the growth starts to flop by midsummer. In addition, they are below ground for five or six months, leaving your garden unattractively empty and open to weed colonization. Do you really need them?

hybrid roses

Hybrid roses, including the large-flowered and cluster-flowered types, have to be pruned every year, to keep them in shape and promote lots of new flowering growth. They have to be regularly deadheaded, to make sure that there's more than just one flush of flowers. They need regular fertilizing if they are going to flower well, while they offer little leaf growth that'll cover the soil and prevent weeds growing around them. Hybrid roses are also notoriously susceptible to attacks by pests and diseases, particularly blackspot and mildew.

bedding plants

Seed-raised annuals might give an incredible display, but they are short-term displays. They must be dug up and discarded when they die, the soil has to be prepared for the next intake, and the bedding plants have to be grown from seed or bought as young plants. Then you have to plant them, as well as fertilize and water them regularly, to maintain a good show of flowers. And all this must be repeated several times a year. Instead, choose reliable shrubs that will look after themselves and offer interest in every season.

10 no-fuss shrubs

These plants are handsome, reliable, and need little attention. They remain attractive and perform well with little or no pruning.

1 *Berberis* x *stenophylla* (barberry)

2 *Choisya ternata* (Mexican orange blossom)

3 *Cornus alternifolia* 'Argentea' (pagoda dogwood)

4 *Cryptomeria japonica* 'Elegans Compacta' (Japanese cedar)

5 *Elaeagnus* x *ebbingei* cultivars

6 *Ilex* x *altaclerensis* cultivars (holly)

7 *Mahonia* x *media* 'Charity'

8 *Potentilla fruticosa* cultivars (shrubby cinquefoil)

9 *Pyracantha* 'Orange Glow' (firethorn)

10 *Viburnum plicatum* f. *tomentosum* 'Mariesii' (Doublefile viburnum)

take your time

If your garden is taking too long to maintain and you want to swap your high-maintenance, fussy plants for the easy-care kind that will fend for themselves, don't do it in one go. Gradually remove the difficult plants, replacing them as and when you are ready. And if you dream of a virtually gardening-free future, stick to shrubs. They will eventually block out all the neighboring perennials, leaving you with a relatively work-free shrub garden.

8 care-free bulbs

Bulbs are the ultimate easy-care plants, many coming up year after year and producing a wonderful display of vibrant flowers, without requiring any attention. Choose reliable plants with neat foliage, so you won't need to tidy them up as they die down.

1 *Anemone blanda* (Grecian windflower)

2 *Chionodoxa luciliae* (glory of the snow)

3 *Crocus tommasinianus*

4 *Cyclamen hederifolium*

5 *Galanthus nivalis* (common snowdrop)

6 *Muscari armeniacum* (grape hyacinth)

7 *Narcissus* cultivars (daffodil)

8 *Scilla siberica* (spring squill)

quick fix decorative mulches

Organic mulches, such as compost, are fundamental in the no-work garden, suppressing weeds and keeping the soil moist. Inorganic mulches can play the same role, and there are many stylish, decorative options. Crushed glass, in a range of colors from black to green and vivid blue, is a great choice for a contemporary setting. Silvery gray slate chips make an effective foil for architectural foliage plants in shades of green and blue, while crushed shells add a more traditional note. Spread a layer of the mulch, 3 in. (8 cm) deep, over the garden soil.

2 ideas to minimize work

stay off the soil

When you tread on the soil it will become compacted and so will require digging up, to loosen it. To prevent the need for this chore, avoid stepping on the soil altogether. There are two ways to do this. First, arrange a series of strategically placed stepping stones throughout the garden, to stand on while tending plants. Second, keep your beds less than 4 ft. (1.2 m) wide, which will allow you to reach all parts of it without having to step on the soil.

reduce the flower garden

Plants are clearly the most time-consuming element in a garden, so if you want to keep work to a minimum, reduce the area for the flower garden. Even easy-care shrubs need some work, so try doing away with some of them or limit their size. The flower garden can be replaced with a hard surface, such as pavers or gravel, or with a lawn. If you feel the need to make up for the lack of plants with other attractions, add garden ornaments and statues, vertical features, such as arbors and arches, or specimen trees and shrubs.

8 drought-resistant shrubs

Frequent watering is time consuming and a waste of water. Choose plants that are naturally resistant to drought and that will happily withstand dry conditions. Keep them moist after planting, though, until they have settled in well.

1 *Aucuba japonica* 'Crotonifolia' (Japanese laurel)

2 *Cistus* x *purpureus* (rock rose)

3 *Cytisus* x *praecox* 'Warminster' (Warminster broom)

4 *Escallonia* 'Langleyensis'

5 *Hebe* 'Great Orme'

6 *Ilex aquifolium* (English holly)

7 *Lavandula angustifolia* (lavender)

8 *Rosmarinus officinalis* (rosemary)

slowly does it

Fast-growing shrubs soon outgrow their space and need to be cut back regularly, to stop them blocking a path, obscuring a window, or squashing neighboring plants. Instead choose slower-growing shrubs that won't need constant trimming. If the garden looks bare at first, plant some clump-forming perennials, such as hardy geraniums, among the shrubs to cover the soil while you are waiting for them to grow.

10 bulbs for a bold statement

Some bulbs have a big personality. Simply pop them in the soil and wait for the flowers.

1 *Allium cristophii* (ornamental onion)

2 *Allium giganteum* (ornamental onion)

3 *Crinum* x *powellii*

4 *Fritillaria imperialis* (crown imperial)

5 *Galtonia candicans* (summer hyacinth)

6 *Iris* 'Blue Magic'

7 *Lilium regale* (regal lily)

8 *Lilium speciosum* (lily)

9 *Tulipa* 'Apeldoorn' (tulip)

10 *Tulipa* 'Blue Parrot' (parrot tulip)

3 ideas to avoid trouble

avoid the thugs

Vigorous spreaders, such as comfrey, mint, some euphorbias, and some of the cranesbills, don't belong in the no-work garden because you will be forever keeping them in check and untangling them from other plants. If a plant does start to spread rampantly through your garden, dig it up and get rid of it. It is important to choose plants of similar vigor when they are next to each other, so that they all have an equal chance of survival and so that you don't get weak ones being bullied by their more vigorous neighbors.

avoid the fusspots

Just as it makes sense to avoid over-vigorous plants, it is also wise to avoid weaker plants that need special attention and might even fail to grow well. Stock your garden with easy-care plants—those that are not susceptible to pests and diseases, don't need pruning or cutting back to flower well, don't need staking to stand up straight, don't need protection in cold weather, and that tolerate drought without curling up and dying. Plants that don't do well are a waste of garden space, look unsightly, and use up valuable time.

stop the self-seeders

Some plants, such as aquilegias and fennel, are attractive and well behaved. That is until they set seed. To avoid digging up hundreds of seedlings, enjoy the flowers and then cut off the seedheads before they get a chance to scatter their load.

8 great grasses

Grasses are wonderful plants that are reliable and easy to care for, perfect for the no-work garden. All you need do is cut off the dead stems in early spring. Bamboos are equally easy but might need occasional thinning.

1 *Briza media* (common quaking grass)

2 *Carex oshimensis* 'Evergold' (sedge)

3 *Cortaderia selloana* 'Pumila' (dwarf pampas grass)

4 *Festuca glauca* (blue fescue)

5 *Hakonechloa macra* 'Aureola'

6 *Miscanthus sinensis* 'Zebrinus' (zebra grass)

7 *Phyllostachys nigra* (black bamboo)

8 *Stipa gigantea* (giant feather grass)

save time get it right first time

When planting your garden, be sure to choose plants that you know will do well in it. Check the plant labels to make sure that you can provide the right amount of sun or shade, dryness or moisture, and so on. If your neighbors are growing camellias and rhododendrons, you'll probably also have acidic soil, in which case stick to plants that thrive in such conditions. Avoid any impulse buys if you can't be sure they'll thrive in your soil.

choosing easy-care perennials

Herbaceous perennials can be a fussy lot: most require cutting back in the fall or spring, and some need propping up as they grow, to prevent them flopping all over the place. Instead choose plants, such as lambs' ears (*Stachys byzantina*), lady's mantle (*Alchemilla mollis*), or brunnera, which form spreading mats of foliage so that they cover the ground and suppress weeds. Alternatively, use the likes of sedums or acanthus to form neat clumps of fairly low-growing, self-supporting foliage. Also look out for evergreen perennials, such as bergenia, ajuga, and London pride (*Saxifraga* x *urbium*), which don't need cutting back.

10 care-free perennials

These plants are tough and will grow well in a range of different situations.

1 *Acanthus spinosus* (bear's breeches)

2 *Ajuga reptans* cultivars (bugleweed)

3 *Alchemilla mollis* (lady's mantle)

4 *Anemone* x *hybrida* hybrids

5 *Bergenia cordifolia* (elephant's ears)

6 *Brunnera macrophylla* (Siberian bugloss)

7 *Geranium* 'Johnson's Blue' (cranesbill)

8 *Heuchera villosa* 'Palace Purple' (coral flower)

9 *Kniphofia* cultivars (red-hot poker)

10 *Nepeta* x *faassenii* (catmint)

quick fix
easy roses

The vast majority of roses require far too much attention for the no-work gardener (see pages 24 and 112). Shrub roses, however, are reliable plants that don't succumb to disease and don't require deadheading or regular pruning. They may not produce such perfect blooms as the large-flowered bush roses, but the trade-off is well worth it. Look out for *Rosa* 'Geranium' (a hybrid of *R. moyesii*), *R. rugosa* 'Rubra', *R.* x *alba* 'Alba Maxima', *R. glauca*, and *R. gallica* 'Versicolor' (also known as *Rosa mundi*).

8 drought-resistant perennials

Grow plants that withstand drought so you don't have to water them in dry weather. Even though these plants don't mind dry soil, be sure to mix in plenty of organic matter when planting, as that helps retain moisture in the soil, and the plants will definitely benefit.

1 *Echinacea purpurea* (coneflower)

2 *Echinops ritro* (small globe thistle)

3 *Eryngium alpinum* (alpine sea holly)

4 *Liriope muscari* (big blue lilyturf)

5 *Saxifraga* x *urbium* (London pride)

6 *Sedum* Herbstfreude Group 'Herbstfreude' (stonecrop)

7 *Sisyrinchium striatum*

8 *Stachys byzantina* (lambs' ears)

3 shrubs that really earn their keep

Mahonia japonica

This handsome, upright shrub has fine, architectural qualities and makes a great specimen plant, growing up to 6 ft. (2 m) tall. Its spiky, glossy foliage is arranged in open rosettes, and, being evergreen, it gives an attractive, year-round display. From late fall to early spring, when there is little else happening in the garden, it produces large sprays of primrose-yellow flowers with a gloriously heady scent. The flowers are followed by striking, blue-purple berries. Other mahonias are also reliable plants.

Cornus mas 'Variegata'

A bushy shrub, growing up to 8 ft. (2.5 m) tall, this dogwood is a reliable all-rounder, with something to offer in every season. At the start of the year, in late winter, spidery, yellow flowers appear on the bare branches. In spring, the pretty leaves appear, fresh green with smart, white margins. In late summer, lots of bright red fruits develop, which is why this plant is also called the cornelian cherry. And, in the fall, the foliage has beautiful, red tones as it falls.

Viburnum tinus 'Gwenllian'

A lovely, evergreen shrub, growing up to 10 ft. (3m) tall, this makes a rounded mound of glossy green foliage. In late winter and spring, the plant is covered by a profusion of dark pink buds that open into lacy heads of dainty, pink-white flowers. Masses of dark blue-black fruits develop after the flowers, giving the shrub an extra season of interest.

easy-care planting styles

minimal planting

Minimal planting means fewer plants, and that means less work. It can also mean a stylish, chic look, but the plants that are used must really earn their keep. Choose architectural plants that make a bold statement and benefit from being used alone: you don't want nearby plants detracting from their shapes. Think: cordylines, phormiums, trachycarpus, and other spiky subjects; straight uprights such as *Juniperus communis* 'Hibernica'; or fountain shapes, such as many of the ornamental grasses.

groups and drifts

A group of plants with the same needs will take less time to care for than a garden full of different plants, and the design can be very impressive. For example, plant a narrow border in full sun with a line of lavender plants and they'll bush out to fill the space and make a magnificent mass of silvery foliage, with a profusion of fragrant flower spikes in summer. A shady garden can be filled with large drifts of cranesbills, interspersed with drifts of London pride (*Saxifraga* x *urbium*), to provide winter interest.

quick fix groundcover shrubs

These shrubs offer the perfect solution for suppressing weeds and reducing maintenance, but aesthetically they often leave a little to be desired. However, with some imagination, groundcover doesn't have to be a dull carpet of boring green. Why not mix several shrub species together, to create a pleasing contrast of leaf or flower color, but check that they are equally vigorous, so that they grow at the same speed. You could also create a colorful tapestry of different heaths and heathers in a sunny spot or mix ivies with different leaf colors and shapes in a shady corner beneath some trees.

10 groundcover shrubs

These plants have a dense, spreading habit and block out any weeds. Be sure to check the correct planting distances so that you aren't left with any gaps between them where weeds can sprout.

1 *Calluna vulgaris* cultivars (Scotch heather)

2 *Cotoneaster dammeri*

3 *Erica carnea* (winter heath)

4 *Euonymus fortunei* cultivars (wintercreeper)

5 *Hebe pinguifolia* 'Pagei'

6 *Hedera hibernica* (Atlantic ivy)

7 *Hypericum calycinum* (rose of Sharon)

8 *Juniperus squamata* 'Blue Carpet' (juniper)

9 *Mahonia repens* (creeping mahonia)

10 *Viburnum davidii*

groundcover perennials

Many low-growing, mat-forming perennials make a very effective, dense carpet of growth that'll cover the soil beneath larger feature plants and prevent weeds emerging. Lambs' ears (*Stachys byzantina*) makes a dense carpet of furry, silver leaves, while ajugas come in shades of green and purple. And there are cultivars of deadnettle (*Lamium maculatum*) with handsome, green, yellow, or silver leaves, perfect for a wide range of different color schemes. To keep the foliage dense and fresh, remove the flower spikes of all these plants as they appear in spring and summer.

12 groundcover roses

These roses have been bred specifically to spread and cover the soil with dense growth. Many flower well over many weeks, and they need little attention other than the odd shear over if they become straggly.

1 'Essex' (pinkish-red with white centers)

2 'Flower Carpet' (deep pink)

3 'Grouse' (white blushed with pink)

4 'Hampshire' (scarlet)

5 'Kent' (white)

6 'Laura Ashley' (pink and lilac)

7 'Nozomi' (very pale pink)

8 'Pink Bells' (bright pink)

9 'Robin Redbreast' (dark red)

10 'Snow Carpet' (cream-white)

11 'Swany' (white)

12 'Tall Story' (pale yellow)

creative conifers

Conifers are made for easy-care gardens: they are tough and reliable, available in a range of colors and forms, and won't need pruning if you choose the right plants for your garden. They are excellent for mixing with deciduous plants, to create a year-round structure. Conifers come in shades of gold, bronze, green, yellow, and blue, while the shapes include prostrate, rounded, and columnar. Check the eventual height and width before you buy. You don't want to spend time cutting them back, and they rarely look good when they have been hacked, no matter how sensitively.

10 care-free conifers

The following conifers offer a range of colors and shapes that can be used as bold design features, and to contrast with or complement other plants.

1 *Cedrus deodara* 'Aurea' (deodar cedar)

2 *Chamaecyparis lawsoniana* 'Chilworth Silver' (lawson false cypress)

3 *Chamaecyparis obtusa* 'Nana Aurea' (hinoki cypress)

4 *Juniperus* 'Grey Owl' (juniper)

5 *Juniperus scopulorum* 'Blue Heaven' (Rocky Mountain juniper)

6 *Picea glauca* var. *albertiana* 'Conica' (dwarf Alberta spruce)

7 *Pinus mugo* 'Mops' (dwarf mountain pine)

8 *Taxus baccata* 'Dovastonii Aurea' (English yew)

9 *Taxus baccata* 'Fastigiata' (Irish yew)

10 *Thuja occidentalis* 'Rheingold' (American arborvitae)

2 plants for groundcover in shade

Geranium macrorrhizum

Cranesbills form leafy cushions of soft green, aromatic foliage that is so dense it makes good groundcover. This vigorous species is semi-evergreen, with the leaf cover thickest in summer, thinnest in winter, and with attractive, orange-red tints in the fall. In early summer, the plant is covered with clusters of pink or white flowers. 'Ingwersen's Variety' has soft pink flowers, while 'Bevan's Variety' has darker, crimson flowers. Many other hardy geraniums also make good groundcover, including *G. himalayense*, *G. nodosum*, and *G.* x *riversleaianum*.

Pulmonaria officinalis

This pretty, evergreen leafy perennial is grown both for its attractive foliage and its flowers. It forms dense mats of low-growing, bright green leaves with attractive, white spots. In early spring, lots of little, funnel-shaped flowers open rich pink, then turn purple, and then blue as they fade. Plants in the Cambridge Blue Group have pale blue flowers, while the hybrid 'Sissinghurst White' produces very spotty leaves and white flowers.

decorative details

quick fix
plastic lining

Porous containers, such as terra-cotta and ceramic, dry out much more quickly after watering than containers made from nonporous materials, such as plastic. To reduce the time spent watering, line porous containers with plastic, before adding the potting soil. Also make a few drainage holes in the base, to allow excess water to drain away, and tuck the top of the plastic below the soil surface, to hide it.

save time
easy
watering

Reduce your watering regime for containers by mixing some water-retaining crystals into the potting mix, at planting time. When they get wet, these crystals swell up and store the water until it is needed. As the potting mix around them becomes dry, the water is gradually released and the mix stays moist for longer.

encourage natural predators

Many of the creatures that visit your garden offer a helping hand in the battle against pests, and you can encourage them to come more often, even with just a small pond. Birds, turtles, frogs, and toads are all voracious eaters with a penchant for plant-eating aphids, slugs, snails, and other annoying pests. Give them somewhere to drink and bathe, and they will be happy to stick around.

give them access

Make sure your garden pond is accessible to all the helpful, pest-eating creatures by making a shallow bank at one end of the pond or by providing shallow stone steps down into the water. This will make a big difference to the number of creatures you attract. It is also a good idea to have some foliage cover around at least one side of the pond, to allow shy creatures to get in and out as they wish.

2 things to avoid

alpine gardens

The traditional alpine garden—a pile of dirt with rocks randomly sticking out—is a gardener's nightmare in terms of maintenance. Weeding is near impossible, as invading weed roots become established between and under the rocks, and they will be virtually impossible to get out without dismantling the whole feature. It gets even worse if the alpine garden adjoins a lawn without any form of mowing strip separating the two, as it is impossible to mow right up to the bottom tier of rocks. If you want to grow alpine plants without all these problems, construct a simple raised bed from railroad ties or other pieces of pressure-treated lumber, filling it with gritty soil and rocks for good drainage. If you make the walls of the raised bed from rocks, mortar them in place, then add a mowing strip if the bed adjoins a lawn.

lots of little containers

Small containers dry out very quickly and need watering at least once, if not twice, a day in warm weather. Missing a day or two of watering in midsummer can decimate the contents, so do you really need that kind of responsibility? The situation is especially bad if you have lots of little containers dotted about the garden, making watering a fiddly and time-consuming task and increasing your chances of forgetting some of them. Hanging baskets and small window boxes are especially needy, as they quickly dry out and require regular watering. Ask yourself whether your containers are really essential, and whether you'd miss them if they weren't there. If the answer to both questions is "No," get rid of them right away.

quick fix
shed
makeover

It is rarely possible to hide away utility features, such as the garden shed, especially in a small yard. Screens and strategically placed shrubs often only serve to draw attention to the area you are trying to hide. Instead, why not make it attractive in its own right and include it in the overall garden design? With a speedy coat or two of paint or colored woodstain, you can transform a tired, old shed into something very special. Choose soft sage-green or lilac for a muted, contemporary feel or dark green for a formal setting, perhaps with a few parts picked out in gold. If you are really adventurous, use bright pastel colors to make the shed look like a beach hut, and it'll be ideal for a gravel garden. Let your imagination run wild: you can easily repaint it when you want a change.

don't bend down

Raised beds give easy access to plants, and even weeding isn't that daunting when you don't have to bend. They also make more of a special feature than a border and are ideal for getting your nose close to short, scented plants. You can even grow trailing plants to spill out of the soil and down the walls. Build the beds out of brick, stone, pressure-treated lumber, or old railroad ties—whichever suits your garden.

quick fix
add a
topdressing

To improve the look of raised beds, pots, and alpine gardens, and to help reduce weed growth at the same time, apply a topdressing of gravel or grit. Simply add a layer 1 in. (2.5 cm) deep on top of the soil, and it will prevent weed seeds below from germinating by blocking out the light. It also sets plants off nicely and gives a neat, well-tended appearance to the garden.

easy-care garden furniture

aluminum

Aluminum furniture needs no maintenance and is lightweight, making it easy to move around the yard. It is also inexpensive and comes in a range of stylish designs. Keep in mind that the very contemporary look may not suit every garden style.

hardwood

Chairs, tables, and benches made from oak, teak, or other tropical hardwoods always have a classic elegance that suits most garden designs. If you choose good-quality furniture it should last for many years without requiring any maintenance. It will last even longer if you can protect it over winter by storing it in a shed or covering it with a waterproof tarp. Make sure the wood comes from a renewable source.

plastic

Plastic furniture is cheap to buy, and some of it is very attractive. It is often more comfortable than other garden furniture and is light and easy to move around. The colors tend to fade if the furniture is left out all year, so cover it over winter or choose white. Plastic chairs, tables, and loungers often stack one on top of another, making them easy to store.

2 ideas to reduce watering

keep out of the wind

Containers will dry out far more quickly if they are placed in an exposed, windy site. In fact, wind will dry plants out much faster than sunshine. Try to set containers out of the wind, to reduce the need for watering.

automatic irrigation

If you have a number of containers and little time to spend on them, install an automatic irrigation system, leaving you free to do something else. A drip system is ideal: a narrow, flexible pipe runs from the faucet, with smaller pipes branching off it into the tops of the containers. The system can be controlled with a timer, so you don't even have to remember to turn it on. Simply set it up to come on for a short time each evening, and the watering is done.

leaf-free ponds

If you are planning to create a pond in your yard, take care where you site it. Don't position it under overhanging trees or close to large shrubs, unless you are prepared to cover it with a net; otherwise, when the fall arrives, you will have to spend hours fishing leaves out of the water. If you don't remove them they will rot and upset the balance of the pond, eventually causing the water to turn green with algae, creating another problem, which will take time to sort out. In any case, most aquatic plants prefer an open, sunny site to grow well; they become leggy and drawn in shade and do not flower readily, so a bright, open spot is preferable for them too. Don't forget that even evergreen trees drop their leaves—they just do it throughout the year rather than all in one go. Yew trees (*Taxus*) can be a particular problem for pond fish, because their berries are toxic.

save time automatic garden lights

When choosing garden lighting, select models that come on automatically so you don't have to switch them on every evening. There are two choices. First, the solar-powered lights that come on automatically as it gets dark, and you don't have to lay any cables. Many last for up to ten hours if they have been fully charged during the day, and more attractive designs keep coming onto the market. Second, there are lights that are triggered by a movement detector, and they automatically switch on when they are needed. They are convenient, energy saving, and good for security.

low-voltage lighting

If you are using electric-powered garden lights, choose a low-voltage system, as it will be quicker and easier to install. If you use standard household current (120 volts), the outdoor lights have to be installed by a professional electrician, and the devices have to be protected by a circuit interrupter. In a low-voltage system, a simple step-down transformer, which reduces the current to 12 volts, is plugged into a standard electrical socket in the house, and the low-voltage cables that run to the lights outdoors do not have to be buried but can simply lie on the soil surface. Low-voltage kits can be installed without a professional, and so are cheaper.

8 easy-care pond plants

These well-behaved plants are ideal for a small pond. Don't be tempted by impulse buys unless you know how much the plants spread.

1 *Aponogeton distachyos* (water hawthorn)

2 *Caltha palustris* (marsh marigold)

3 *Hottonia palustris* (water violet)

4 *Iris laevigata* 'Variegata' (water iris)

5 *Myriophyllum aquaticum* (parrot feather)

6 *Pistia stratiotes* (water lettuce)

7 *Pontederia cordata* (pickerel weed)

8 *Typha minima* (dwarf cattail)

bigger is better

If you have decided you definitely need some containers in your garden, use the largest you can afford. Larger containers dry out much more slowly than small ones, requiring less watering. And because they contain more potting soil, they give plants more space to grow and can contain more nutrients, leading to stress-free, healthier plants that will look better and need replacing less often, saving you time and effort. Large containers can also make a bold, striking feature, eliminating the need for surrounding plants. Since even empty, large containers can be quite heavy, make sure there's someone to help you move them around your garden. Plastic containers, looking like terra-cotta or lead, are a good, lightweight alternative.

quick fix
pond plants
in baskets

Using aquatic baskets for your pond plants, instead of rooting them in the soil at the bottom of the pond, gives easier access to them if they need thinning or tending. Just lift them out and put them back when you have finished. Baskets also offer the advantage of restricting the growth of more vigorous plants and prevents them spreading madly. Choose baskets at least 9 in. (23 cm) wide, to give plants space to grow, and line them with burlap, to prevent the soil falling out. Always arrange the baskets at the correct depth in the pond, to suit the plants. Most marginals like to have 3½–6 in. (8–15 cm) of water above them, but others prefer more. Just follow the notes on the plant labels. If necessary, stand the baskets on bricks, to raise their height.

2 ideas for style without work

border edgings

Border edgings are quick to create and need no further maintenance, yet they can add great style to a garden. There are many different types available, from rope-edged terra-cotta and decorative cast iron to low wicker hurdles and sheet lead edgings with attractively shaped tops. Choose whatever takes your fancy, or create your own, using rounded stones or scallop shells inserted vertically into the soil.

garden ornaments

Statues and sculptures can increase a garden's style, and should be chosen and positioned with care, for maximum impact. Since you'll have to live with them for a long time, make sure that they really do give you pleasure. Large, grand ornaments are best placed in an open area, where they can't be missed, making effective focal points. Smaller, quirkier objects, like old, cracked pots, can be very effective half nestling among plants, giving a sense of faded grandeur.

water without the work

If you like the sight and sound of moving water, but don't have the time to make or care for a garden pond, install a pebble fountain, using a simple kit. The water typically bubbles up through a hole in a millstone or a similar object, then drains into a hidden reservoir beneath, before being recirculated by a pump. A wonderfully relaxing addition to a small garden or seating area, it's also perfectly safe for young children.

avoid fish

Unless your pond is large, don't introduce fish as you will have to feed them regularly in the summer months. You'll also have to introduce some oxygenating plants to keep the water and the fish healthy. Fish can also upset the natural balance in the pond and encourage algae that feed on fish waste and turn the water green.

2 ideas for easier containers

easier fertilizing

Remembering to fertilize the plants in your containers on a regular basis is a chore. During summer, while they are in full growth, container plants need fertilizing every week. Doing this with a liquid fertilizer can be very laborious and time-consuming. Instead, use slow-release fertilizer pellets, which will last for weeks. They can be forked into the surface of the soil.

easier hanging baskets

Hanging baskets notoriously dry out very quickly, so they're not a good choice for the no-work garden. However, if you really like them, choose a self-watering basket with an in-built water reservoir. Fill it up when you water the basket, and the potting mix will stay moist for far longer than in a standard basket, which needs watering twice a day in warm weather.

save time
pack it away

Pack away garden furniture, barbecues, awnings, and other accessories over winter to make them last longer, saving you the job of cleaning, painting, renovating, or, at worst, replacing them next spring. If you don't have space under cover, buy some good-quality tarp, to keep things dry and protect them from bad weather. You can even buy waterproof covers specially designed to protect chairs, barbecues, tables, and hammocks from the rain. It is a good idea to stand the items on a hard surface, for example a patio or deck, because if they're on grass or dirt there will be extra humidity inside the covers. If storage is a problem, choose chairs that stack neatly together or the fold-up kind that close up for storing in the garage or shed.

lazy containers

Many containers are attractive in their own right and look striking even when empty, making them ideal no-work garden ornaments. Look for containers with an unusual shape, such as urns with narrow necks or wide, shallow bowls. The more decorative and distinctive the pots the better, if you want to use them unadorned, although very simple pots can look good in a minimalist setting. Look out for terra-cotta designs, which can be very decorative and highly patterned, or choose bright glazed pots, to add color.

unusual fillings

Pots and containers don't have to be filled with plants—there are other interesting options that don't require any maintenance at all. Fill wide, shallow bowls with pretty stones or a selection of shells, or choose colorful ground glass mulch or glass beads, for a contemporary setting. Taller pots can be filled with handsome twigs, striking bamboo stems, or even a collection of walking sticks. Use your imagination to save you work.

save time go solar

Installing pond pumps and lights are jobs for a professional electrician and can be expensive, so go solar. Solar-powered devices don't need installing and can be up and running quickly. They might not be as powerful as some electric models, but they give decent results and come in different styles, some with integral panels, others with larger, free-standing panels. The lights are available as underwater or floating models.

small pond, small plants

In favorable conditions, aquatic plants can grow very quickly, and some species are liable to fill a small pond in no time and choke out the other plants. This applies to marginal plants as well as the submerged oxygenators. Choose pond plants according to how much space you have in your pond, avoiding very vigorous species such as cattails (*Typha latifolia*), unless you have a very large pond. If you introduce these thugs you will have to reduce their spread several times in the growing season, and it will be very difficult to get rid of them, especially if you allow them to root in the pond rather than confining them in a container.

quick fix
simple but
effective

A shrub in a pot can go a long way toward enlivening a dull patio or deck and needs very little maintenance. Choose one that'll really earn its keep. Leafy, architectural shrubs look good all year, and the best include clipped boxwood or yew, cabbage palms, colorful spiky phormiums, and hardy yuccas. For a shrub with several attractions, try a skimmia with its handsome, evergreen foliage, spring flowers, and red berries, or an evergreen viburnum that bears attractive flowers and berries. Pick a pot to enhance your shrub, making sure that it's in proportion to the plant and is large enough to provide adequate space for its growing roots, with plenty of soil and nutrients to keep it happy, without any fussing for several seasons.

retail therapy

Colorful accessories can transform a bare square of patio with a simple table and chairs into a funky yard—it's all in the shopping. Clever shopping is a great way to make a no-work garden, as you'll need little in the way of plants and other features if you use a selection of bright accessories to add color and interest. Pick a theme or color scheme and stick to it when choosing all of your accessories for the most harmonious effect. This is the perfect scenario if you like entertaining but don't have time for gardening.

• Tablecloths and napkins are an easy addition for instant color. Fabric, paper, and plastic cloths all come in bright patterns and designs, from retro to cutting-edge. Buy a selection to use as the mood takes you or for different occasions, such as summer lunches, early evening cocktails, or a formal dinner outside.

• Cushions are as easy on the back as they are on the eye. There are plenty of outdoor designs from which to choose, but there's no reason why you can't pick out some stylish interior cushions as long as you move them in when rain threatens. Choose rich silks or velvets for evening use, cheerful chintz or cottons for daytime.

• Don't forget the finishing touches, in the form of candles, wind chimes, vases of flowers, or bowls of attractive pebbles or shells to add character.

save time group them together

Container care is easier and less time consuming if all the pots are grouped together. In addition, they'll create a moist microclimate, which will help prevent the potting mix from drying out so quickly, while offering more favorable growing conditions for the plants.

10 drought-resistant container plants

Choosing plants that are naturally drought resistant means less watering and gives the plants a fighting chance if you do occasionally forget to water them.

1 *Calendula officinalis* (pot marigold)

2 *Erigeron karvinskianus* (fleabane)

3 *Hedera helix* cultivars (English ivy)

4 *Ilex aquifolium* 'Argentea Marginata' (English holly)

5 *Lavandula angustifolia* (lavender)

6 *Pelargonium crispum* 'Variegatum' (geranium)

7 *Pelargonium* cultivars (geranium)

8 *Sedum spectabile* (showy stonecrop)

9 *Sempervivum* cultivars (houseleek)

10 *Thymus vulgaris* (common thyme)

10 easy-care container plants

These plants are solid and reliable, perfect for easy-care containers.

1 *Acer palmatum* cultivars (Japanese maple)

2 *Camellia japonica* cultivars

3 *Cordyline australis* (New Zealand cabbage palm)

4 *Cynara cardunculus* (cardoon)

5 *Miscanthus sinensis* cultivars (eulalia grass)

6 *Nepeta* x *faassenii* (catmint)

7 *Phyllostachys nigra* (black bamboo)

8 *Rosmarinus officinalis* (rosemary)

9 *Saxifraga* x *urbium* (London pride)

10 *Viola* cultivars (pansy)

easy edibles

save time
container-grown edibles

Containers are perfect for growing vegetables.

- The first big advantage is that you don't have to do any digging.

- Weeding is almost nonexistent, because you'll be using bags of sterile potting mix without any dormant weed seeds.

- Fertilizing and watering are easily managed, producing first-rate crops.

- It's easy to give your crops the potting mix they like best. You might have heavy, lumpy clay in the garden, which is slow to warm up in spring, but conditions in your pots will be exactly right.

quick fix
too much of a good thing

To avoid having a glut of vegetables, sow just a few seeds of each crop, such as lettuces, beet, and radishes, at a time, then sow another batch a few weeks later, and another a few weeks after that. This successional sowing staggers your harvest, giving a steady flow of fresh food over several months.

5 seeds for sprinkling

These plants are easy to grow and quick to mature. Simply sprinkle a few seeds into a patch of bare soil or a container, and enjoy the results a few weeks later. Harvest the plants while they are young, so you don't need to bother thinning them. Carrots and beets are especially sweet and delicious if they are eaten while small and tender.

1 Beets

2 Carrots

3 Radishes

4 Salad greens

5 Scallions

choose disease-resistant edibles

When selecting seeds or young plants, pick varieties that are resistant to pests and diseases, and then you won't need to spend time treating sick plants. For example, the carrots 'Flyaway' and 'Sytan' are resistant to carrot rust fly, the parsnip 'Gladiator' withstands canker, and the bush bean 'Cantare' is unaffected by viruses. Check the varieties when you buy, and you'll be rewarded with healthy plants.

gorgeous gooseberries

For easy-grow fruit, try gooseberries. They start fruiting well in their second year, when they'll be the first soft fruits of the season. They are happy in sun or partial shade, and thrive in a large pot, and these are varieties that aren't fussy about the soil and don't get viruses. 'Careless' is delicious and grows in a range of soils, 'Jubilee' is resistant to virus, and 'Invicta' is a heavy cropper that doesn't get mildew.

quick fix instant results

Grow bags are the ultimate easy option. You simply cut a slit in the top of the bag, pop in the seeds or young plants, and water well. Place the bag at the base of a sunny fence or wall, and then you can attach vertical strings from the top to the grow bag, letting the vines grow up it. Look out for peat-free grow bags, to save the environment.

3 all-time easiest edibles

zucchini

Zucchini are vigorous plants. One plant gives a steady stream of delicious fruits throughout summer, and two will keep a family going. Sow two seeds in a small pot of all-purpose potting mix in late spring, stand it on a windowsill, and keep moist. If late seeds germinate, discard the smaller seedling. When the seedling is large enough to handle, plant it out in the garden or into a larger container, adding extra organic matter. Keep watered. The more you pick, the more the plants produce. Throw the plant away in the fall.

radishes

Radishes are the ultimate in easy edibles. Sow a few seeds, and you could be pulling your own radishes four weeks later. Radishes grow fast and need to be harvested as soon as they are ready, or they become tough and woody. Sow the seed in a container or a patch of bare soil in the garden in late spring, and keep just moist. When the roots have swollen, pull up the entire plant by the leaves and sow the next batch. Look out for red, pink, purple, and white varieties.

bush beans

Bush beans, such as kidney, snap, and lima beans, are easily grown and you won't even need to provide supports if you choose dwarf varieties. In addition to green varieties, there are also purple, red, yellow, and white-flecked ones. Sow seeds *in situ* in late spring and keep well watered, especially when the plants are in flower. Harvest the beans while they are still small and tender. The more you pick, the more the plants produce. Discard the plants at the end of the season.

save time
restrict
your mint

Although it is invaluable in the kitchen, mint is a bit of a thug in the garden and spreads at an alarming rate. By the time you realize what's happened, you'll be spending hours with a spade slicing it back. To prevent it from running unchecked, grow mint in a bottomless bucket sunk in the soil. Make sure that the bucket is deep or the roots will escape out of the bottom.

quick fix
easier
strawberries

The easiest way to grow strawberries is in containers where you can provide the ideal potting mix. Use a mixture of soil-based potting soil and well-rotted compost or animal manure. Pest prevention is also much easier in a container: use special slug tape around the pot, to create a barrier against slugs and snails, and throw a small piece of netting over the top, to keep off birds. It is equally easy to keep the moisture levels just right to prevent mold and mildew: water only when the potting mix starts to dry out.

attract beneficial hoverflies

Hoverflies are invaluable as they lay their eggs near colonies of aphids, and the emerging larvae promptly eat the pests. To attract more of these useful predators and keep your vegetables free from attack, grow the poached-egg plant (*Limnanthes douglasii*). Hoverflies prefer plants with open flowers, which make it easier for them to get to the pollen. Sprinkle a few poached-egg plant seeds in your garden, and you'll soon have a spread of bright yellow flowers. When the plants start to fade, shake out the seeds into the soil, and you'll get an even larger colony next year.

grow only the best

Most people have limited time and space for growing vegetables. If you want to try just a few home-grown edibles, pick those that are far superior to their supermarket equivalents. Home-grown tomatoes, for example, are far sweeter and more delicious than anything you can buy, because commercial crops are picked before they are ripe, to increase their storage potential. Other crops, including peas, asparagus, and corn, start to lose their sweetness as soon as they are harvested, so the quicker you can eat them, the tastier they are. Limit yourself to the real winners: tomatoes, peas, beans, zucchini, and baby carrots.

quick fix
whiteflies
deterrent

For generations, gardeners have been growing French marigolds among their tomato plants, because they prevent whiteflies attacking the crop. Some even claim that tomato plants grow better and produce more fruit if there are marigolds close by. Whiteflies can be a serious threat to many greenhouse crops, particularly tomatoes and fuchsias, but they also attack brassicas outdoors. The little, sap-sucking insects can weaken and even kill plants. There are several theories as to why marigolds keep whiteflies away. It has recently been discovered that French marigolds attract hoverflies, whose larvae kill the whiteflies. However, some gardeners believe the pungent smell of the marigolds masks the inviting smell of the tomatoes; others that the yellow flowers attract the pests away from the tomatoes. Whatever the reason, it works, so buy a few young French marigold plants and grow them among your tomato plants for an aphid-free summer.

save time
choose the right container

Most vegetables need to be kept in constant, steady growth to produce a good crop. If moisture levels are erratic then leafy crops, such as lettuce, spinach, and leeks, will be ruined, as they instead produce flowers and seed, and fruiting plants, such as tomatoes, will split when they get a large drink after a dry period. So, when you are growing edibles in containers, be sure to choose pots that retain maximum moisture, to prevent the soil drying out and to cut down on the time spent watering. Choose glazed or plastic containers, and stand them in a saucer of water in very dry weather. Inexpensive, plastic containers are the most practical option, but choose attractive, glazed pots if they are going to be placed in a prominent spot, for example on a deck or patio, and line them with plastic.

2 ideas for easier edibles

chard

True spinach is notoriously fussy. It needs very fertile soil with a high nitrogen content and plenty of organic matter and must never be allowed to dry out. It will also start producing seed in warm weather, when the leaves promptly lose their flavor, making all your efforts worthless. Chard, however, avoids all these problems and makes a fine substitute. It doesn't go to seed and is a tough plant that will withstand exposed, windy conditions. Sow seed in fertile soil in early to midspring for a summer crop, or in late summer for winter harvesting. Pick the leaves from the outside as you need them and, if the plant looks tired, cut off all the foliage. It will quickly resprout with fresh leaves.

single-stem apple trees

Apples are probably the easiest fruits to grow. Choose single-stem trees, as they form a compact column of growth and need little pruning. They are perfect for growing in containers and can be grown in a tight space. Look out for 'Ballerina' and 'Minarette', which reach about 6 ft. (2 m) high. Avoid the hard-work, standard apple trees, which have to be pruned once or twice a year, depending on the variety, to create the right fruit-producing framework.

2 more easier edibles

alpine strawberries

If you want hassle-free strawberries, choose alpine varieties. These pretty, perennial plants produce plenty of sweet, little fruits from midsummer through late fall. Although the fruits are smaller than those of June-bearing strawberries, the flavor is better and has a wonderful, aromatic sweetness. Pests and diseases aren't a problem, nor are slugs, snails, and birds. Alpine strawberries thrive in the garden and in pots, and they don't need special treatment.

fall-fruiting raspberries

Fall-fruiting raspberries will produce fruit in their first year. The crop may be a little smaller than summer raspberries, but the maintenance couldn't be simpler. Just cut off all the stems in early spring. The most popular variety is 'Autumn Bliss', but look out for 'Golden Everest' with sweet, yellow fruits. Unlike summer raspberries, fall-fruiting ones don't flop or need tying to posts and wires.

3 perennial edibles

globe artichoke

Perennial globe artichokes are so impressive they can be grown in the flower garden. They form a large rosette of enormous, spiky, silver leaves from which flower spikes 3 ft. (90 cm) tall shoot up in early summer. You actually eat the flower buds, and they should be harvested before they open, starting at the top of the stem. Plant in a sunny spot, and keep the roots moist by applying a mulch in spring.

rhubarb

Rhubarb will grow almost anywhere, and a single plant will produce enough delicious, pink stems for the whole family to enjoy year after year. Plant in a sunny spot in the garden, and mulch with organic matter, to enrich the soil and keep it moist. Don't harvest any stems the first year, to allow the plant to get established. The following spring, and every year thereafter, pull off and eat about half the stems, but stop harvesting in midsummer, to allow the plant to grow.

European Welsh onion

European Welsh onions are rather like giant chives, and they make a good easy-to-grow substitute for scallions. They are an important ingredient in Chinese and Japanese cuisines. They actually come from Siberia and can easily survive the harshest winters without needing any care. Plant in the garden and pick the leaves when needed. Look out for 'Welsh Red', a good hardy variety that is very useful.

herbs for the no-work garden

Many herbs are easy, reliable perennial plants so they make a great choice if you want to grow some edibles without creating too much work for yourself. Fresh herbs are invaluable in the kitchen and can transform your cooking. Most herbs can be planted in the garden or in containers, and they require no more attention than any other plants. They are, in fact, ornamental in their own right and have the advantage of edible leaves.

• Rosemary, thyme, and sage are all handsome, evergreen shrubs that look good year-round. As a bonus, they come from Mediterranean areas and are naturally resistant to drought, so they won't require time spent watering in dry weather.

• Chives, marjoram, tarragon, and oregano are also perennial plants, which make pretty additions to the flower garden and require no special attention.

• Parsley and chervil are biennials, which flower in their second year and die. They are, however, fuss-free plants and worth the small amount of extra effort required. Buy small plants each spring, harvest the foliage as you need it, and discard the plants after they flower the following year, replacing them with new ones.

• Plant comfrey and mint with caution, as they can be rampant and spread quickly.

10 easy-care herbs

These easily grown perennial herbs make attractive additions to the garden and produce plenty of foliage for the kitchen.

1 Bay

2 Chives

3 Fennel

4 Lemon balm

5 Marjoram

6 Mint

7 Rosemary

8 Sage

9 Thyme

10 Winter savory

quick fix
do away with the veg garden

Try growing your edibles in the flower garden between ornamental plants. This gives incredible flexibility. If you don't want to grow many crops one year, simply grow flowering plants instead. You'll also have far less digging and weeding if you adopt an easy-care soil regime. Compare this to a dedicated vegetable garden, which has to be tended year-round, regardless of what's growing in it, and won't always look good.

grow them well

When deciding which of the tempting array of edibles to grow, be realistic and choose just a few different types. It is much better to select a limited number of varieties, and grow them well, than try all sorts of different fruits and vegetables when you haven't got the time or space to care for them properly.

choosing lettuce

When deciding which lettuce to try, select looseleaf varieties rather than heading types, as they are much less demanding. Looseleaf varieties can be grown as cut-and-come-again crops (cut off the foliage when the plants are still small, and they will produce another crop of leaves), or you can simply harvest individual leaves from the plants as you need them. The most popular looseleaf lettuces are 'Salad Bowl' (a lovely, curly green variety), 'Oak Leaf' (a handsome plant with brown-tinged foliage), and 'Lollo Rossa' (the well-known, red variety). Heading lettuces need far more water and fertilizer and are liable to produce seed, when the leaves turn bitter.

keep them happy

The best way to protect your fruit and vegetables from pest and disease attacks is to keep them in optimum health by fertilizing and watering regularly. Keep the soil fertile by regular mulching with organic matter, and add extra fertilizer in the form of all-purpose fertilizer or well-rotted compost or animal manure for hungry crops such as zucchini. Organic matter will also help the soil to retain moisture, though you'll still have to give plants a drink in dry weather.

8 edibles for growing in a container

Most fruit and vegetables can be grown in a container, but these are especially successful.

1 Apple trees, column varieties

2 Beets

3 Hot peppers

4 Zucchini

5 Lettuce

6 Peppers

7 Pole beans

8 Tomatoes

get the balance right

Cottage-style gardeners of old knew a thing or two about protecting their vegetables from marauding pests. By growing a wide selection of different plants, they attracted a good range of insects to the garden, both predators and prey. This meant that nature dealt with any infestations of pests. To do the same, choose a varied range of plants, and mix vegetables and ornamentals in the same areas. Be sure to include some indigenous species that will attract all sorts of beneficial insects.

quick fix
instant color

If you feel your vegetable garden could do with a little color, plant a few nasturtium seeds. Simply pop them into the soil and a few weeks later you will be rewarded with bright, sunny, orange and yellow blooms on handsome, leafy stems trailing between your other plants. Both the flowers and leaves of nasturtiums are edible, so use them to pep up salads.

save time
buy young
plants

The quickest, easiest way to grow vegetables is to forget about doing it yourself. Go out and buy them as young plants and put them straight into your garden or containers. There are far more varieties available in garden centers than several years ago, so keep an eye out for tasty tomatoes, cucumbers, peppers, zucchini, eggplants, corn, melons, and "slips" of sweet potatoes. This saves a huge amount of time spent sowing seed, trying to provide the right temperature, transplanting, finding space under cover for great piles of propagation trays, worrying, and fussing.

3 things to avoid

vigorous fruit trees

Large, vigorous fruit trees soon get out of hand in a small yard, and even in a larger space it is very difficult to prune them and harvest the fruit without a ladder and a lot of spare time. The ultimate size of a fruit tree depends on the rootstock onto which it is grafted. There are dwarf and semi-dwarf rootstocks to keep fruit trees in check and limit their size, to 8 ft. (2.5 m) and 12 ft. (4 m) respectively. Avoid standard rootstocks, which will grow considerably higher.

strawberries in open ground

Strawberries are fussy plants that need well-drained, moisture-retentive soil with plenty of organic matter. If they get too moist or dry, they are prone to gray mold (*Botrytis*) or mildew, and it is hard to control soil moisture in the open garden. The foliage rots if it gets too wet from overhead watering or too much rain, and they need straw tucked under the fruit to keep them off the soil. They are also prone to attack from slugs, snails, and birds.

veg gardens with rows of plants

A traditional vegetable garden, with plants growing in long rows with bare soil between them, is an extremely high-maintenance feature. All that bare soil is a magnet for weeds, and if you tread on it you'll have to fork it over, to avoid compaction. Sections of it will also have to be manured and fertilized every year. Instead, grow vegetables in small, narrow beds, which can be reached from the paths, and plant close together to suppress weeds. The individual vegetables may be smaller, but the overall yield will be higher.

save time keep them close

For convenience, plant herbs within easy reach of the kitchen so that they're handy when you want a sprig of mint for your potatoes or a handful of rosemary for a casserole. Grow them in a small patio bed, in a container, or in a special raised bed next to the barbecue so they are within arm's reach when you are cooking *al fresco*.

give them what they need

Soil and exposure are important considerations when it comes to growing fruit and vegetables, and make a huge difference to the quality and quantity of the crop. They also greatly affect how well a plant will deal with a pest or disease. For example, blueberries require acidic soil and perform very badly in alkaline conditions. And peaches need warm, sheltered conditions, being best planted against a wall that faces the midday sun. Give the edibles the conditions they need for the best results.

index

Page numbers in *italics* refer to illustrations.

acknowledgments

Publisher: Jane Birch
Senior Editor: Charlotte Macey
Deputy Creative Director: Geoff Fennell
Design: one2six
Production Controller: Carolin Stransky
Picture Researcher: Janet Johnson
Picture Librarian: Taura Riley

PICTURE ACKNOWLEDGMENTS

Alamy Albaimages 103; Andrea Jones 189; Elizabeth Whiting & Associates 153; ISP Photography 151; John Glover 161, 211; Martin Hughes-Jones 81; Susie McCaffrey 137; Suzanne Long 69; Wildscape 223.
Andrew Lawson 17, 21, 196; Design: Christopher Bradley-Hole, RHS Chelsea 2004 40; Design James Aldridge 119; Design: Patrick Wynniatt-Husey & Patrick Clarke Hampton court Flower Show 2000, 193.
Clive Nichols 57.
Corbis Mark Bolton 19; Derek St Romaine 33.
GAP Photos Abby Rex 61, Clive Nichols, Design: Kathy Taylor 165; Clive Nichols, Design: Geo Designs 42; Clive Nichols, Feibusch Garden, San Francisco 155; Clive Nichols, Hedens Lustgard, Sweden 217; Clive Nichols, Design: Clive Nichols, Location: Rickyard barn Northants 171; Elke Borkowski 25, 63, 73, 99, 107, 175; Friedrich Strauss 179, 183, 213; Graham Strong 191; Howard Rice, Design: Toby & Lisa Buckland 7; J S Sira 177; Janet Johnson 85; John Glover 141, 203, Design: Judith Glover, Chelsea flower show 2003 55; Jonathan Buckley 13, 113, Design: David Chase 157, Jonathan Buckley Design: Jean Goldberry, Catalyst Television 23, Jonathan Buckley West Deans Gardens Sussex 227, JS Sira HCFS 2005 Design: Paul Hensey 11; Leigh Clapp 187; Leigh Clapp, Design: Green Dot Gardens 159; Leigh Clapp, Location: Spurfold 53; Lynne Brotchie 125; Marcus Harpur 127; Nicola Browne 199; Pernilla Bergdahl 95; Rice/Buckland 83; Richard Bloom 185; Richard Bloom, Location: Foggy Bottom, Bressingham, Norfolk 145; S & O 110; Zara Napier, Location: Parsonage House, Essex 15.

Garden Picture Library Botanica 131; Frederic Didillon 93; Friedrich Strauss 37; Howard Rice 207, 215, 225; John Glover 65,133; Mark Bolton 147; Mel Watson 79; Michael Davis 8; Pernilla Bergdahl 219; Richard Bloom 121; Steven Wooster, Design: Anthony Paul 59.
Garden World Images Nicolas Appleby 209.
Getty Images S & O 67 Marcus Harper,Design: Zoe Cain for St Joseph's Hospice RHS Chelsea Flower Show 2008 UK.
istockphoto.com Andrey Volokhatiuk 49; William Walsh 31.
Janet Johnson 105, 143, 201, Design: David Sorrell 29.
Marianne Majerus Design: Ward and Benard 181; Paul Southern 163.
Octopus Publishing Group Limited 101, 123, 129, 135, 229, 231; David Sarton 46, 169, 221; Freia Turland 109, 197; Howard Rice 45; Marcus Harper 77, 91, 97; Mark Bolton 51.
Photolibrary J S Sira 173; Mark Winwood 38.
Shutterstock Joanna Wnuk 71; ppl 27.
The Garden Collection Jonathan Buckley, Demonstrated by Alan Titchmarsh 89; Jonathan Buckley, Design: Bunny Guinness 35; Liz Eddison 148, 205; Liz Eddison, Design: Aughton Green Landscapes 74; Liz Eddison, Design: Walter Dall'Omo - Hampton Court 2005 117; Michelle Garrett 87; Nicola Stocken Tomkins 113, 233.